Lynn is the mother of seven children, five sons and two daughters. A New Jersey resident all her life, she calls the Jersey Shore her home.

Lynn and her husband, Albert, had been members of St. Justin's Church and the Light of Life Prayer Group for over 40 years. This experience of living in the Spirit changed them and their family in remarkable and dramatic ways.

Lynn provides unique and practical insights of raising seven children in this humorous memoir. Scripture and tales from her own distinctive childhood are included in this *Raising Seven*.

In memory of my husband and best friend Al DeAngelo. "Children are a heritage from the Lord, offspring a reward from him.

Like arrows in the hands of a warrior are the children born in one's youth."

Ps. 127: 3-4 NIV

And dedicated to our seven loving children

Tom, Brian, AJ, Matt, Jon, Christine and Melissa

Lynn DeAngelo

RAISING SEVEN

My journey with God

Patty,

Enjoy & Be Blessed

Lynn De Angelo

1 Corn 13:13

AUSTIN MACAULEY PUBLISHERS™

LONDON • CAMBRIDGE • NEW YORK • SHARJAH

A CIP catalogue record for this title is available from the British Library.

ISBN 9781398410428 (Paperback)
ISBN 9781398410435 (ePub e-book)

www.austinmacauley.com

First Published 2022
Austin Macauley Publishers Ltd®
1 Canada Square
Canary Wharf
London
E14 5AA

Special thanks to my son, AJ, for encouraging me from the very beginning, always aimed at pushing me forward. Even purchasing me a book for me on how to write a memoir. He was my biggest supporter and personal go to tech guy. I would also like to express my gratitude to my niece, Kellyann, for her early editing skills, especially in helping me decide what comes first. My sister, Kathy, a published author herself, helped submitting manuscripts and her searching out publishing companies was invaluable. Also, Kenny, a family friend who read my very first draft and affirmed my writing and story-telling skills. Most of all told me not to get discouraged. Lastly, I want to acknowledge my baby sister, Gerry, not only for her time, patience, and expertise, but also for the endless days and hours of editing, proofing and printing the whole manuscript.

Table of Contents

Chapter 1

The Past/Present

Paradise Fishing Lake

It was in 2009 when I first thought about writing my memoir. My son AJ gave me a book for Christmas that year, entitled *Writing the Memoir* by Judith Barrington. It inspired me to write and I began to do the exercises in the book, and I found that I really enjoyed writing. Life gets busy. Working full time and being a wife and mother meant writing this memoir was put on a back burner. It wasn't until an interaction with a stranger in the summer of 2011, when I knew the memoir absolutely had to be written.

I was watching my husband, Al, fishing at Paradise Trout Hatchery in Paradise Valley, PA. I always bring a book on vacation, and on this warm sunny morning, I sat reading one of my favorite mystery novels at the old wooden picnic table. The table was resting on a small hill facing the crystal-clear blue stream where Al fished. As the sun shone warm and bright, I squinted into the light as an elderly black gentleman approached me in his fishing gear and said, "I see you are a writer."

I smiled and said, "Well today I am a reader, and maybe someday I will be a writer."

As he passed by me, he gently touched my shoulder and said, "You have to get started on that memoir."

As he continued down the narrow hill, I thought, *Wait! What just happened? Who was that man?* Well, I thought to myself, *I am in Paradise Valley, and maybe things like this happen in paradise.* This was my 'epiphany moment' when a complete stranger tells me to get moving on writing a memoir. Not a book, not a short story or some random crazy idea, but a memoir! My secret to myself; I realized the Holy Spirit revealed it to him at that moment, I knew then it was God's will to write my memoir.

"Lord, you have probed me, you know me; you know when I sit and stand; you understand my thoughts from afar. My travels and my rest you mark; with all my ways, you are familiar. Even before a word is on my tongue, Lord, you know it all."
Ps 139:1-6

I have many pictures of my family in our living room. Surrounding these pictures, I placed sayings such as, *Cherish Yesterday, Celebrate Today* and *Dream Tomorrow*. But I really feel we must live in the present. I read somewhere, "Yesterday is history. Tomorrow is a mystery. Today is a gift. That is why we call it 'The Present'". (attributed to Elizabeth Roosevelt) It was an insight about the nature of time which really touched me and played a part in the writing of my memoir.

The present is a hard one now for my children and me. My husband, Al, passed away during the writing of our story on December 7, 2012. He had a successful open-heart surgery in late November. The day before he was due to come home, Al began having difficulty breathing. That evening, his cardiologist put him back on oxygen and early the next morning he collapsed in the bathroom. I was sitting in his hospital room writing out our Christmas cards, when I heard him fall. I ran out to the nurse's station for help. When Al regained consciousness, the staff lifted him back onto the bed, and fired questions at him left and right. Did he feel dizzy, was he nauseous? I was standing outside his hospital room door, when I heard him say, "I cannot talk and breathe at the same time." This kind of common-sense remark was something we were all familiar with, it was so much like Al! His last words made me smile. The head nurse called me back into the room, I had no idea this would be the last time we would be together. As his eyes rolled back, and he took his last breath, the head nurse yelled, "code blue!" *and* I was rushed out of the room.

I sat calm and confident in the waiting room with a minister the hospital called; it was comforting to have someone there with me. As I spoke with the minister, I shared that I was sure Al would be fine, after all, I reasoned; Al made it through open heart surgery, he'll make it through this too.

His heart surgeon came out 45 minutes later and said that they have done everything to bring him back.

I just looked at him in disbelief, finally exclaiming, "Are you saying he is gone?" With sadness in his eyes, he confirmed Al had passed. I was completely blindsided. I never thought he would not make it. It was later determined a blood clot had been the cause.

When I visited Al earlier that morning, he shared with me that when he received Eucharist that day, he felt a great connection with Jesus. As he shared this with me, he was in awe of the experience and spiritually moved by it. Just a few short hours later, Jesus took him home to heaven. I think of that often. I am so thankful that a Eucharistic minister came that morning to Al, and Jesus was so present to him.

It was a few days later that I recalled the evening before he passed. Al and I took a walk into the sitting area for visitors. He stood with his back to the wall, and I remember looking up at him and thinking he looked different. He looked taller and thinner; I even remarked to him that I thought he'd looked like he lost weight. Even his face somehow looked different; his eyes, as he scanned the room, had a serious look. I recall turning around to see why he was looking around the room that way.

I knew that look but could not place it at the time. The year before, Al copied and framed a picture of Jesus from the book, *Heaven Is for Real.* The story of a young boy who dies and comes back from heaven. This young boy points out a sketch of Jesus drawn by a young girl, who also experienced death and heaven, before being brought back to life. The boy claims that sketch is what Jesus really looked like. I realized after Al passed, that was the look that I saw on Al's face that last evening.

"All of us, gazing on the Lord's glory with unveiled faces, are being transformed from glory to glory into his very image by the Lord who is the Spirit."
2 Corinthians 3:18

It was my faith that got me through those first days and it continues to get me through each day. I know where Al is now and his spirit is still alive in my heart.

The most difficult time was having to tell our children their father did not make it. I made the calls from the hospital visiting room with the help of Al's surgeon. He spoke to a few of our children after I had told them the news. He did his best to explain, in a compassionate manner, what happened to their father. I remember thinking how difficult it was; thinking everything was okay and suddenly life changes dramatically.

When I think of Al not being with us any longer, sadness comes over me. But it is those times that Al lets me know in many funny ways he is here in spirit.

"When we love, and lose someone, they are not where they were before, they are now wherever we are."
Saint John Chrysostom

For example, the first Christmas without Al, the whole family went to the cemetery on our way to have dinner at my son's house. As we pulled into the grounds on that cold overcast day, I told my daughter Christine that we should sing a song. She suggested we sing Al's favorite song *Dominick the Christmas Donkey*! I said "No way!" We prayed The Lord's Prayer, and climbed back into our cars. As Christine turned on the ignition, *Dominick the Christmas Donkey* started blasting from the radio! We laughed and laughed, "Ok, Dad! We hear you. Have a Merry Christmas in heaven."

Another time, while driving Al's Ford Expedition, James Taylor's verses, 'I've seen fire and I've seen rain, and I thought I would see you again' was playing on the radio. As I pulled into the driveway, I said, "Yeah, Al, I thought I would see you again too." As I exited the car, the alarm went off, which never happened to me before. However, it would happen to Al many times when he locked the doors on the Expedition. I would always ask, "How do you do that?"

He would laugh and say, "I don't know, my thumb gets in the way."

That was a first for me, and it never occurred again.

Anytime the kids or I see a rainbow we think of that cold clear sunny morning as we made our way to the cemetery after Al's funeral Mass. High up in the clear blue sky was a rainbow, it was beautiful and bright as could be, yet very strange. Instead of a bow shape rainbows usually have, it was oblong. We all made comments on this unique rainbow as we drove behind the hearse. As family and friends exited their cars to go to the burial site, they pointed to the rainbow and started laughing. I said, "Come on, give Al a break…it's his first rainbow!"

There will be loving reminders of the wonderful man who left this life too early. Some called him 'Big Al', his seven children called him dad, while others knew him as Professor DeAngelo or Uncle Al. He will always be the love of my life, my best friend, and yes, the man who made all my dreams come true. Those dreams all began a long time before we met. As a young girl growing up, I always played house with my dolls, a mom's heart even back then.

Chapter 2

Early Years

Me with my sisters and my mom on a porch

My earliest memories of my childhood began in Bayonne, New Jersey where I was born. I had one older sister by three years, Patricia, named after my mom, and two younger sisters, by five years known as 'the twins', Kathleen and Geraldine. My parents didn't know they were having twins till they were born. So, only having one name Kathleen that they picked if they had a girl, they went with a rhyming name, Geraldine. Then there was me, Lynn. The middle child.

Speaking of names, my baptismal certificate records my name as Marie Lynn. This is the only place the name Marie appears. In 1945, you had to have a saint's name to be baptized. Marie was my mom's younger sister's name, Where here my parents got Lynn from, they never did tell me! I believe it was the Lord who put that name in their hearts.

"The Lord called me from birth; from my mother's womb, he gave me my name."
Is 49:1

My birth certificate from the hospital states Lynn. When Catholics make their Confirmation, they again need a saint's name; I chose Denise. Today all my documents read Lynn Denise. Today it's a joke with my kids, they tease me, "Hey Mom! What is your real name?"

As I said earlier, my mom didn't know she was carrying twins during her pregnancy, surprise, surprise! I was five years old when they were born, I raced to answer the phone when the hospital called to tell my dad; he became the father of twin girls. Husbands at that time were not allowed to be a part of the delivery as it is today. I will never forget that phone call. I ran into his bedroom, jumping on his bed, waking him up, "Daddy, Daddy, Mommy just had twin girls, the hospital just called!" Of course, he didn't believe me. Twins? Girls? Two? Nooo.

When we moved away from the city of Bayonne, New Jersey, I was ten years old. I will never forget that bitter cold day in November 1955. So cold that our fingers became numb, even with gloves, as I helped move the lighter boxes into our new house. What a change from a garden apartment in the city to a brand-new home in the country! How excited we all were that day. Our first home in Union Beach, the beach town where I did all my growing up, till I married. Our home was in a development called Haven Park. Haven Park was on the outskirts of the town. Closer to the beachfront, you found large older homes and a few bungalows dispersed throughout the area. The streets were not paved anywhere in Union Beach and there were no sidewalks except in Haven Park; we literally walked the block and a half to the little red brick schoolhouse.

The model we purchased was a split level. We had a flight of stairs up to the two bedrooms. One bedroom was for our parents and the master bedroom was for the four of us. We had a full bathroom at the end of the hall where the four of us would all crush together doing our hair and makeup when we got older. The half bathroom downstairs had a toilet and where the washer and dryer lived.

My mom went to work for the first time, but she had to learn how to drive. Yikes! That was scary. My dad would take all four of us kids with him to teach her how to drive. Since the car was a stick shift and not an automatic, mom learnt to use a clutch shift, as we rolled backwards down a hill, in the middle of traffic! We all screamed for our lives in the backseat. We survived and mom got her license and first full-time job!

Patty and I became the main caretakers, babysitters and entertainers. A thirteen-year-old and a ten- year old were in charge of each other and the twins. Most of the time I was the one who entertained the twins. This was for two reasons; one, I had a great imagination, and second, I didn't have a choice. Patty being thirteen, she would disappear with her friends for hours at a time. I was happy Patty wasn't there; she could not boss me around and make fun of my made-up games. We didn't have computer games to play, so we did a lot of pretending and playacting. Since I had a wonderful imagination, I made up many unique and fun games to entertain Kathy and Gerry while we were home alone.

They will tell you that I was also the one who would scare them for my *own* entertainment! I also would write plays, and when our parents came home, we would put on a performance. We would also gather our friends in the yard and come up with tricks and make-believe high wire acts etc., which we called THE CIRCUS. Everyone had some talent to show off. We invited our neighbors and the parents of our friends to be the audience. Later when my own children were little, I did the same thing with them and their neighborhood friends. It wasn't really a circus this time, but more like a talent show. And long before *America Has Talent*!

I never thought watching my sisters was a burden. We had a lot of fun. I would invite my girlfriends over and we would play games like 'Hide and Seek' in the house. We would re-arrange all the furniture for hiding places. My very best friend Elaine and I would dream up all kinds of imaginary games. Our sofa would become a boat and we would be sailing out in the ocean, calling for help. When we did this, the twins would get

ened and we would laugh hysterically. At the end of our playtime, ver was over at the house would help me straighten up. They would help me get the dinner ready; peeling potatoes and setting the table. is the rule! And Elaine would help me enforce it. I really didn't know re Patty would disappear to, but she was hardly ever home.

In the summer, both of us were to babysit. Patty would tell me, "You ve the morning to go out and be back by noon to babysit." Since she as older and bigger, I did what she said or she would torture me if I didn't! Telling on Patty was not something I did. She would make sure she got even with you when our parents were not home, and it would not be pleasant. We were all afraid of Patty.

Me and my childhood friend Elaine

When I think about it now, it was just easier for me to invite my friends over than try to go anywhere and be back by noon. On the flip side, my friends and I had a place to talk and laugh. Call boys on the phone, even play with our cut-out paper dolls. There was no one to tell us what to do, or what not to do—we did what we wanted. We would play Elvis records and dance all over the house. My childhood was a happy one, for me anyway. Today, DYFUS would be called on parents and be arrested for leaving children watching children. This was our life during the 1950s in the Rooney house.

Chapter 3

Falling in Love

My wedding photo

The summer before my 21st birthday, I rented a large home in Seaside Park, NJ with my girlfriends from Western Electric. Summers in New Jersey can be very warm and humid, and we were all very excited to rent a home near the ocean. The cool breezes off the ocean would cool off the heat of the day, and a few drinks at the shore clubs didn't hurt us either. The Jersey Shore was a great place to spend the summer with my co-workers. We called the house *The Yellow Submarine*, yes it was yellow! We loved the Beatles; well half of us did.

This is where I met Al, who would become my husband two years later! The summer of '66 was one of the best I can remember. The warm sunny lazy days, no parents, just five girls who worked together, getting away on weekends and our vacation days.

The house had two bedrooms on the first floor, a full bath, a huge kitchen with a round colonial style table; with big comfy floral cushioned chairs. It was here we entertained most of the time. The front entrance opened up to a small but welcoming furnished living room. Upstairs was a small half bath, and two large bedrooms. There were rafters that supported a pitch roof; the bedrooms were dormitory style. We all agreed that if anyone's boyfriend was staying over, they would have the downstairs bedrooms and the other girls would share the upstairs bedrooms.

This all sounded very good when we planned it, but those upstairs bedrooms were HOT! Did I mention no air conditioners anywhere in the house? We all wanted the beds that was near the windows, so we could feel those cool breezes at night.

We also had house rules. One was, no closed bedroom doors when the guys were visiting. The girls would supply the food (we took turns shopping) and the guys supplied the adult beverages. That was the best rule!

On weekends we would go to the Surf Club in Ortley Beach. We enjoyed their private beach; swimming, sunbathing and drinking. Waitresses would come directly to your beach chair from the club bar, taking your order, making it very convenient and easy to sunbathe and drink. The evenings there were always busy. Music, dancing, laughing a little more than flirting! The entertainment was great live bands and Go-Go girls dancing in cages! The drinking age in 1966 was the same as now, 21. I wasn't twenty-one yet, but I had an ID that said I was 23. My older sister Patty was able to lend me her driver's license as there were no photos IDs like there are today.

One Saturday night in August, my girlfriend Betty came for the weekend to visit as my guest. The guy she was dating, brought my future husband Al DeAngelo with him to the Surf Club. Al was from the Italian section of the city called The Berg. I can't say it was love at first sight, but we had a lot of fun together and I definitely liked him. At the end of the evening, Betty and I invited them over the house for coffee; we talked for hours, getting to know each other better. They probably left at 4 am to drive back to Trenton. Yet, they both came back Sunday afternoon unexpectedly and met us at the beach. We had not made any plans with them, plus Trenton is about an hour away from the beach.

As we are coming out of the ocean, after an hour of riding waves and totally enjoying ourselves; here we are soaking wet hair, no make-up, and we spot both of them on the beach looking for us! We didn't know if we wanted to hide from them or wave! Betty said, "Oh no, they are here!" Too late now to worry about how we looked! They had driven all the way back to Seaside and they came looking for us, it was what I call now, a 'divine' appointment. So, we took our chances! And what a chance it was for Al and me, it was a 'whirlwind courtship'.

That September, Al was just beginning his postgraduate work towards his master's degree in Aquatic Biology at Rutgers University. The following year we became engaged on my birthday, 15 September, 1967. Ten months later on Saturday, 13 July, 1968 we became Mr and Mrs Albert J. DeAngelo Jr at St Mary's Catholic Church in Perth Amboy.

And thus, begins my memoir. Our story raising seven children and coming to know Jesus Christ as our Lord God and Savior; experiencing all God's blessings on our family, and the lessons we learnt through trusting in Him. To this day, I am often asked, "How did you do it?" My answer is through God's grace and mercy. Here is the 'How' of our story.

Chapter 4
Our Family in the Beginning

Me with three boys

In the September of 1968, two months after we married, Al started teaching Biology at the Junior High School in Sayreville, N.J. A small town in the northern portion of New Jersey, about thirty minutes or so outside of New York City. I continued working at Western Electric in Kearny, New Jersey with the girls that I shared the summer house with before we married. We all worked together in the office portion of Western, aka the boring 'paper pushing' department. Eventually I put in for a transfer to the TA building, for a more challenging office work and a better salary. I was loving this new position! It was a fun working environment, and the girls there were also a lot like myself, newly married and around my age. During our breaks, we would play a fast and furious card game of spades; trying to fit in as many hands as fifteen minutes would allow. That year I became an avid card player.

By March 1969, I became pregnant with our first child, took a maternity leave and never returned. When I left Western Electric, I had a stock in AT&T that we cashed in. I didn't become wealthy and blessed with loads of money, but we became rich in other ways. God was blessing us with our first child of seven! But at that time, we had no idea.

Tommy was born on a clear warm day in June. He had blonde eyelashes and barely any eyebrows, no hair anywhere, he was so tiny. Three weeks before our first wedding anniversary, Tommy made his appearance.

We named him after my dad, Thomas, and gave him Albert as a middle name, after Al. I thought it was great, naming one child after two important men in my life: my dad and my husband.

Tommy turned one in June and one month later, I was pregnant with my second child. We didn't know if the new-born would be a boy or a girl. No ultrasounds back then. The 'reveal' party was at their birth. In fact, I never knew the sex of any of my children beforehand.

Brian was born Easter Sunday, 1971. The Saturday before Easter was also Opening Day Trout Season. Al was an avid fisherman, so off he went with his best friend Marty to fish the Gorge in Hunterdon County. This was about an hour or more away. As I was out shopping for Easter candy, my water began to leak. I rushed home with Tommy in tow and called my doctor. All I could think of was the worst-case scenario; me having my baby at home with my almost two-year-old assisting me! But the doctor assured me that this was normal and no worries. No worries? Yeah right, no cell phones to reach Al at the fishing stream either. I called Al's dad and he came over to stay with me till Al came home that night. I had no pains, just a slow leak. The following morning was a whole different matter. Labour came quick and rapid. This time we called my dad to come get Tommy. When he arrived a few minutes later, he took one look at me and said, "If I knew you were this far along, I would have brought an ambulance." He was a member of the First Aid Squad.

On the way to Riverview Hospital in Red Bank, a twenty-minute ride, Al drove like a mad man. Passing cars at breakneck speed and speeding through yellow lights. Because it was early Easter Sunday, the traffic was light, thank God. We made it to the hospital in time, however Brian was born with an infection and developed diarrhea. My water had been leaking for over 12 hours causing Brian to be very ill at birth.

The diarrhea pediatrician said that diarrhea in an infant can be fatal. He was transferring Brian to the Neonatal Intensive Care Unit at Monmouth Medical Center due to the infection. The nurse wheeled Brian into my room in his carrier for me to say 'goodbye' to him. Brian looked so small and fragile against the stark white blanket that they swaddled him into. All I could think of was the doctor's words to me, "this could be fatal." It was so scary I cried every day we were apart. As back then, mothers did not go with the baby, they stayed on the maternity floor, it was very depressing and lonely. I couldn't wait to get home and for Brian to be released from Monmouth Medical. Al was running between two hospitals, visiting me to console me, and watching over his new-born son fight for his life.

The good news is Brian recovered after being on intravenous for a few days, since I was home by then, Al and I were able to bring Brian home together. A few years later, when Brian would become lost on us, I always reflected back to the time he was born. He pretty much was off on his own traveling from hospital to hospital. Brian apparently got the 'travel gene' at a very young age!

When we moved into our first home in Toms River, NJ, Tommy was two years old and Brian was seven months. I remember it so clearly; it was one of those sunny but blustery cold days we can get here in Jersey. I can still picture my new kitchen, the way the sun came through the front window over the sink. How it made everything look bright and cheery.

Al and I loved the Jersey Shore, after all it was where we met.

In those early days of our marriage, we attended the Mass regularly at St Justin's Catholic Church, that was at a walking distance from our house.

26

One Sunday, a couple made an announcement from the podium that they were sponsoring a Marriage Encounter for couples in the parish. Couples that had a good marriage but wanted to make it better. As it turned out, we knew a few couples that had made the Marriage Encounter previously and encouraged us to attend. They even offered to babysit!

Count me in, Al on the other hand, needed more encouragement. After speaking with the husbands of our friends, Al was convinced. This was going to be a weekend in Princeton. Since the birth of our boys, we didn't get any alone time before this opportunity.

The weekend consisted of presentations by couples that were married under five years, and others married longer. The topics they spoke on were key in how to make a marriage successful and happy. One of the topics was finance, it was excellent. Learning to listen to your spouse, what their dreams were, and not to judge each other, even if they had feelings opposite from yours.

We would listen to the talks, then go to our rooms and write a letter to each other on our feelings, based on the topic. They called it *10&10*. Ten minutes of writing, then read each other's thoughts, then discuss honestly, really listen to each other, for 10 minutes! It was awesome and eye-opening. Two really big decisions which came from that weekend would change our lives forever.

Al was very happy and content to have his two sons. I, on the other hand, really wanted to try for a girl. During our time of listening, Al realized how strong my heart's desire was for a daughter. It was on this weekend when we both agreed to add to our little family.

The second big change was spiritual, and this was one we both desired. On that weekend, we invited Jesus to be the center of our family. Where was Jesus before? Somewhere far, far, away. We believed He died for us, but He was in heaven, and at church you prayed to Him. This was another realization that I contributed to Marriage Encounter, the need to invite Jesus into our marriage in a more personal way. The desire for the other person's happiness took precedence. Our love grew and we became closer. On the weekend, the presenters would frequently say, "We once believed that marriage was 50/50 proposition, we now know it's 100/100." This is so true, and that is exactly what happened; we became one in many ways. We all benefited from inviting Jesus into our marriage. Our prayer life changed; before we never prayed together, now we were praying as a family.

Well, it took over a year to become pregnant. It didn't happen till we relinquished our desire only to want a girl. When we finally prayed, "Lord Jesus, Your will be done!" *boom!* I was pregnant. Tommy was seven and Brian five years old when I delivered our third son, AJ. He was named after his dad, Albert John III. Now people would ask, "Why did you name your third son after your husband?" As if I knew I would have three.

My father-in-law spoke to me one day about naming my third child after my husband, if it was a boy. I was about six-months pregnant at the time, the pregnancy was so different than the two before. I was convinced this baby was a girl. I told him emphatically, "We are having a girl." But I said to appease him, "If we have a boy, I will call him AJ." Reason being, Al's father was known as 'Bert' and my husband was called 'Al', so to distinguish between them with no confusion, we would call him 'AJ'. Many years later, my father-in-law passed away, AJ was the only son who was the exact same size in shoes and clothing as his grand pop, who had named him.

Now I have three sons all happy, all healthy. However, I was still struggling with the fact that the desire of my heart for a daughter was still very real. When I prayed, I asked the Lord to take away this desire if it was not His will. Could it be that I questioned myself if I just wanted what I didn't have? But every time I would see a little girl, my heart would still yearn for a daughter. All my prayers and self-reflection had not changed my heart. ***"May He grant you what is in your heart and full fill your every plan." Ps 20:5***. Life went on and I put the idea aside, determined to trust in God's will.

Of the three boys, AJ was the most care-free, easy-going happy-spirited child, who grew up the same way. However, he was also the family teaser. Tommy and Brian were happy children too; they were more cautious, they seemed to take life more seriously than their little brother. Although Brian was our biggest 'wanderer'. Just amazes me how children all grow up in the same home, have the same parents, the rules don't change very much, yet each child is unique. Their personalities shine and add to the family's character.

At that time, I had been working at Home Interiors & Gifts. It was a Christian company, founded by Mary Crowley and based in Dallas, Texas. We did home interior displays mostly in the evening, allowing me to still be home with my three children and work. Al was now teaching biology at High School South in Toms River. Since we only had one car, it was a benefit he taught locally, and he was home by 3:30. I would load up our car and drive to my appointments. It was so much fun! Not only making extra money but meeting new people and making friends. The job was very profitable. The company would offer recruiting prizes which I often won. I loved what I was doing. I was offering women home decorating ideas, sharing with them the benefits of working parttime while being able to remain a 'stay-at-home mom'. I won a trip to Bermuda for us, a diamond ring for me and two fur coats! I became a very successful businesswoman. I was eventually promoted to management; life was very good.

Mary Crowley, the founder of Home Interiors, gave me my first Bible. She would have training retreats for the managers, it was like a spiritual retreat as well. They were held in her luxurious home in Dallas or her home in the mountains of Colorado. She was a wonderful Christian teacher and mentor. She would fly all her managers across the U.S at her expense every summer. She did this to get to know us personally and so we could get to know her better. We also received hands-on training from Mary Crowley and she was one of the best! Mary's motto was, 'God doesn't make a Nobody, be Somebody'.

She was a self-made millionaire, who loved and served the Lord. Mary built the company from her garage, while raising her two children as a single mom. She was a role model every woman could learn from and admire.

I was able to attend these wonderful retreats, as Al being a teacher with summers off, would take over for me at home. Then when I returned, he would be back working his summer job. With our family growing there were no full summers off for Al.

After AJ was born in October, I did take a maternity leave. This enabled us to have quiet family time, enjoy the new baby and the holidays: Halloween, Thanksgiving and Christmas.

Christmas at the DeAngelo household that year was a joyous celebration of the birth of Jesus and our new baby Albert John III. By January of 1977, I returned to Home Interiors.

Chapter 5

Conversion

Christmas tree photo

In January 1977, when I returned to work as a unit manager of Home Interiors, that winter would set a record of the most snowfall and artic temperatures. It was a bitter cold day when my co-worker Patty and I still decided to go shopping at the clothing outlets in Kearny, NJ. Afterwards, we stopped at a diner for lunch.

There were four Baptist ministers sitting close enough for us to overhear their conversation on the Holy Spirit. It was in the middle of the afternoon and not many people were in the diner. When we overheard the word 'Holy Spirit', our ears perked right up. They were debating whether the gift of the Holy Spirit should be taught to the senior year or the first year as freshmen at their school. Three of the ministers thought it best to have the teaching on the Holy Spirit in senior year, but Patty and I both agreed with the minister who felt the students needed to learn about the Holy Spirit the very first year of school. As they were getting ready to leave, Patty prompted me to share with them our opinion. I am not usually that brave on my own, but as they walked past our table, I spoke up. With a smile on my face, I blurted out that we had been listening to their conversation. I explained to them that as Catholics we did not fully understand the workings of the Holy Spirit. I did not fully understand the working of the Holy Spirit and what the term 'born again' meant.

After some conversation about our beliefs, they asked us if we would like to pray with them right there in the diner to be *born again*. We all stood, held hands, and one of the ministers led us in their commitment prayer, which was very similar to the Catholic Nicene Creed that I prayed every Sunday at mass. They began by asking, "Do you believe in God the Father Almighty? Do you believe Jesus was born, crucified, died, was buried and rose from the dead?" Yes, I believe!

They asked for our addresses so they could send us pamphlets to learn what it means to be baptized in the Holy Spirit. So, we could understand and live the *born again* experience. We gave them our information, said our goodbyes and went on our way.

After leaving the diner, we didn't really feel any different. I asked Patty if she was going to tell her husband Stan we prayed to be *born again?* She said, "NO!" But I knew I couldn't wait to get home and share with Al what had happened. I knew that Al would be very interested in this spiritual experience. After all, Al went to Catholic schools and I didn't even think he knew what it means to be born again.

After dropping Patty off in Kearney, I got on the parkway heading home. It was now late, and an immense beautiful full-moon shone down on the darkened road. I enjoyed the hour ride home, allowing me to think about the day. Tonight, all my thoughts were consumed with the words I prayed at the diner. I felt as though the knowledge went from my head to my heart. I had an over-whelming feeling of God's love and his Presence was so strong I began to weep. Never had I had this experience before. I begged God to forgive me of my sins. I didn't know if I should pull over and pray, or continue home. I decided to continue home. By the time I arrived, I was composed but excited!

As soon as I got in the door, I immediately began to tell Al what happened to me. He listened, with a big smile on his face, and then kidded with me saying, "If you start speaking in tongues, I will throw you out of our bed." I had no idea what he was talking about then. Al *did* know about being born again and I was soon to learn about this gift of tongues.

I received the pamphlets that were promised, and I poured over them. I could not put them down as there was so much information about the Holy Spirit. After that, I started reading the Bible daily, along with spiritual books to help me learn more about the Holy Spirit, which touched me so powerfully. I can still recall the strong feelings of joy and gratefulness during this time, and still do, to this day. I had more confidence in myself than ever before, I felt like a new person. My experience brought me the most profound peace.

"Let the peace of Christ rule in your hearts, since a member of one body you were called to Peace. And be thankful"
Col 3:15

I read once in my daily devotional, that God doesn't call the equipped, he equips the called. Normally, I would not have the boldness, even if someone prompted me, to speak to strangers in a public place about a private conversation. The Lord gave me the courage to speak up that day, and I believe it was a Divine appointment, an extraordinary day in my ordinary life.

My prayer time was different now, I felt very close to Jesus through His Spirit. I began to journal, keeping notes on how God was speaking to me in the Bible. There were many scriptures that spoke directly to me. I began to feel Jesus' beckoning, the call to a closer personal relationship with Him.

One day shortly after my conversion experience, I was at mass and they announced the Charismatic Renewal was holding a *Life in the Spirit*

Seminar. Al and I had acquired many friends through the Marriage Encounter and a few of them were part of the Renewal and would be teaching the seminar.

The Charismatic Renewal is a spiritual movement in the Catholic Church that focuses on a deeper relationship with the Holy Spirit.

I told Al I really wanted to attend this seminar, but I didn't want to go without him. Our friends would talk to Al and encourage him to attend the seminar, because we would learn more about the Charismatic Renewal and the workings of the Holy Spirit.

One night, Gene Clairbeu and Dominic Mannato, came over our house to share with Al what they experienced when they attended the seminar. We sat at our kitchen table and with the boys tucked into bed they had our undivided attention. They shared their stories and the miracles they received in their lives once they made a commitment to Christ. Dominic shared how his prayer life became more alive and he felt the presence of Christ with him in ways he had never experienced before. Gene and Dominic's sincerity and openness had an impact on Al and me. Hearing their words increased our faith. Al was taught all through grammar and high school by Franciscan Priests, but this was something different. He was hooked. God had a big fishing rod and He sent His best two fishermen to catch Al. When men witness to other men, it's powerful.

> **"Frequent the company of the elders; whoever is wise, stay close to him. Be eager to hear every discourse; let no wise saying escape you."**
> **Sir 6:34-35**

It is incredible how the Holy Spirit will touch each of us in different ways. He meets us just where we are, but He doesn't leave us there. I found people are sometimes afraid of what they may have to give up in order to be born again. It is not about giving things up, it is about receiving God's love, mercy and grace. My life began an exciting spiritual journey.

I did not become a weird religious fanatic. My story is about a normal Catholic girl, who found a friend in Jesus.

34

"John baptized water, but within a few days you will be baptized with the Holy Spirit."

Acts 1:15

Chapter 6
Praying God's Will

New year's eve myself and Al with five children

I found out that when my spiritual conversion began it could not be confined to only my home life. It spilled over into every aspect of my life, including my profession. As a unit manager in a Christian company like Home Interiors, it was a comfortable transition. I would pray before each meeting, read scripture from the Bible and the women and I would continue with our decorating ideas. Meetings lasted for most of the day. I would open each weekly meeting with scripture reading from the Bible. The weekly out-of- town meetings lasted for most of the day and Having to travel over an hour each way meant I was away from home the entire day. As a manager, there were training seminars out of state, constant phone calls, helping my girls with customer service, delivery problems, or just lending a listening ear, giving encouragement.

My three sons were young; Tommy was nine years old, Brian was seven, and AJ was two. The commitment to my position had become a burden as my superiors were pressuring me to get more help at home. I was advised to get child care, housekeeper, and whatever else I needed to do in order to devote more time to my position and the company.

I really loved interior decorating with our top of the line merchandise plus helping women decorate and accent their homes. We also did our own floral design arrangements which was another joy I experienced. There were many good aspects to working for Home Interiors and Gifts. I could also see the benefits for growth in helping my family financially. But I also enjoyed being home with the children. I needed to make a decision. I got on my knees in my bedroom and prayed, I asked the Lord to show me His will. I knew from past experience I needed to pray in faith expecting God to answer me.

"But if any of you lack wisdom, he should ask God who gives to all generously and ungrudgingly, and he will be given it. But he should ask in faith, not doubting, for the one who doubts is like a wave of the sea that is driven and tossed about by the wind. For that person, must not suppose that he will receive anything from the Lord, since he is a man of two minds, unstable in all his ways."
Jas 1:5-8

I did not get a word from the Lord at that time, but I knew my prayer was from my heart and the revelation of His will would come.

About one month later, I realized I was pregnant! Back on my knees, I am praying again, only this time I'm not exactly praying, I am distraught. I asked God "What just happened, did You hear my prayer about my work? I prayed for Your will, for my business, not a baby." I grumbled and groaned, questioning my prayer for about two weeks. I walked around dazed and confused until I finally came to grips with the pregnancy and what was God's will. My prayer now was asking for forgiveness I prayed to be filled with joy, I wanted to be happy because I knew this is God's will for me. That prayer was answered immediately. The joy filled my entire being, like sunshine bubbling up inside. You can't help smiling, it turned my feelings from sadness to happiness. I became excited to bring another child into our family. It was a total turn around, only God could change a heart like He did for me.

I knew what I had to do! I would step down as a manager, go on maternity leave, and when I returned it, would be as a displayer. This was always my favorite position. I could be creative, decorate homes and continue to advise women with enhancing their own decorating skills. No pressure on hiring people to raise my children, clean my house and drive hours to training sessions.

I got into full swing with this pregnancy. I bought every book on breastfeeding, natural childbirth and even joined the "Sharing Moms Group" at the doctor's office. All the moms would meet before and after the babies were born. The women were all ages, some having their first baby, others like myself, having toddlers at home.

Breastfeeding was one topic I had no experience with, since I bottle-fed all three of my children as I was a smoker at that time. I really learnt a lot from the other moms' open sharing. Breastfeeding was becoming popular and surprisingly, I found myself wanting to have the experience. Looking back this too was connected to the joy! There were many groups like La Lecher, who offered free advice on breastfeeding and I took advantage of all information available. Additionally, the nurses at the hospital were a great help in teaching moms about breastfeeding and making it easier for those who chose not to bottle feed.

I gave birth naturally to our fourth son, Matthew, on 17 August, 1979, three weeks past his due date. This was the first time Al was with me in labour and delivery. I would like to tell you it was easy delivery, even with Al at my side, the excellent Lamaze classes with breathing lessons, and a wonderful doctor, no it was labor. Dr Ramondi had to break my water, and it showed that the baby already had a bowel movement and was in distress. During delivery, Matt had breathed in too soon and swallowed fluid. The pediatrician on duty worked on him through the night. It was a very stressful evening for us. When I spoke to the pediatrician the next morning, she said Matt pulled through just fine. I thanked her and the Lord for answered prayer. My big boy weighed over 9 pounds, and we both learnt about breastfeeding!

Matthew was nursing and in between his feedings, I was pumping to have bottles ready for the sitter. I would need these bottles of breastmilk when I returned to Home Interiors part time.

During the last few years, Al and I had become very active in St Justin's Light of Life prayer group. We had come into leadership and held the core meetings at our home and still be able to work parttime and take care of the children. Al and I were both seeking God's will on almost every decision we needed to make. Prayer became a normal part of our relationship.

Father Orsini, a Catholic priest in the Charismatic Renewal had written a book on the Holy Spirits' influence on his life, and he was to be the keynote speaker at Our Lady of Perpetual Help parish in Lavallette, NJ. The church was only a few minutes from our home, and I couldn't wait to hear him speak and meet him in person! Al was also very interested in hearing him speak, sharing my enthusiasm. We made sure we left that night open, scheduled our babysitter, and off we went to hear this well-known Catholic Charismatic speaker.

Part of Fr Orsini's talk was on abortion, which the Supreme Court had recently legalized in its decision: in Roe vs Wade. While Father was speaking, I heard God's voice very clearly, say to me, "*I want to bless you with more children.*" In my mind's eye, I saw three children in a doorway, just the shadow of them. And I thought to myself, *one could be a girl*! It was like God was giving me a choice. I said, "Yes Lord, I want the blessing!"

I turned to Al and whispered in his ear, "Did you hear the Lord speak to you about having more children?"

He said, "No!" with an astonished look on his face.

I said, "Think you may need to pray about it, Al, I heard God speak to me about having more children." I didn't dare go into the actual vision of possibly three children…the three figures in the doorway. He would have passed out right there in church.

Formal picture of my entire family

Sometimes, I have found that the scripture will parallel our lives. For instance, I remembered how the Blessed Mother hearing from the Arc Angel Gabriel who said to her, "***You shall conceive and bear a son and give him*** **the name of *Jesus*" Lk 1:31.** I am not comparing myself to the Blessed Mother in any way, but Joseph didn't get his message until after Mary first said "Yes." That night when we got home, Al did pray about the word I had heard from the Lord and he received a simple, "*Trust in Me.*" And we did, trusting in His Divine Plan for our family.

Matthew was 10 months old when I became pregnant for the fifth time. Being a new nursing mom, I didn't know you could conceive while you were nursing.

"What eye has not seen, and ear has not heard, nor has it so much as dawned on man what God has prepared for those who love him."
1 Cor 2:9

It became clear to me, God's will was not to return to Home Interiors. I gave my notice and this time for good. I was done with working outside the home. More laundry, more night-time stories, but I was very happy to be home with my growing family. The work might have been multiplying but the joy was multiplying too!

I read my Bible daily and the message I received often was that God would fulfil my heart's desire. *"May he grant you what is in your heart and fulfil your every plan."* **Ps 20:5**

We all know what that desire was, after four boys, I was hoping this pregnancy would be a baby girl! We had many hands-on friends from church and Marriage Encounter. They cooked dinners for us after I came home from the hospital, helped with laundry, and were just there for Al and me after the birth of each baby. They also confirmed my own thoughts that they knew God heard my prayer, this baby girl would be the answer. Al and I were so convinced we only chose a girl's name.

My pregnancy with my fifth child lasted ten months! When I was three weeks late, they brought me into the hospital to induce me, but the baby wasn't ready so they sent me home! Today they would do a C-section, not send a three-week over-due mom home. I was depressed and scared. Matthew had been three weeks late too and was in stress when he was born. Everything eventually had worked out with him, but I was going into my tenth month, and now I was almost 36 years old.

One week later, I went into labour. Al was with me in the delivery room when our fifth son was born, Jonathan Mark. He weighed in over ten pounds! I could not believe I didn't have a girl! I remember thinking there must be another baby in there. But no, one big happy baby boy. Al leaned into me on the delivery table and said he had been reading his Bible about David's best friend Jonathan, and he wanted to name our son after him. And so, we did. I think I was in total shock.

The doctor who delivered Jonathan came into my hospital room the following day to see me. He was one of the head doctors in the practice I chose, but not my favorite doctor. He was always in a rush, mostly negative and had a grouchy personality. He confirmed that, Jon was a ten-month baby, and in his personal opinion, I should not have any more children. He said I had "an old womb, and one strong uterus" that carried this baby, but I should not have anymore children. I needed to digest this. It was his personal opinion, not his professional one. I didn't ask for his opinion, and I didn't need to hear it. I am glad God was in charge, and not this doctor.

During my stay in the hospital, I tried not to let anyone see me cry. My son was born, and he was very healthy, but that day I lost a baby girl. I felt duped by God, he tricked me! I couldn't even pray to Him anymore. I could only pray to the Blessed Mother, this was not about 'loving' Jonathan, but grieving the 'loss' of a daughter. I loved my new son, I nursed him, and marveled at his size. In the nursery, he looked three months old compared to the other babies. My sisters took all the girl clothes I had purchased and replaced them with boy's clothing before we came home from the hospital. They were a great help to me, both physically and spiritually. Time heals all wounds and soon I was able to see my error. God did not make a mistake. He calls forth life, **"Presently we see indistinctly, as in a mirror…" 1 Cor 13:12**

My family and close friends understood what I was feeling. Love for my new-born son, and at the same time, struggling with the loss of the daughter I didn't have. There were also the people who would mock me. "Oh, you had a boy? I thought God told you it was a girl?" Yeah, people can be cruel, those same people made comments to Al and me about having so many kids. We never regretted having our children, today they are my richest blessings.

I was nursing Jonathan while Matthew would sit next to me on the sofa. I would be reading him a book, multitasking, nursing was becoming second-hand now. Everything was well in the DeAngelo home. Jon was ten months old when I found out that I was pregnant yet again. Some lessons I guess are harder to learn than others! Jon was sleeping through the night, and my menstrual cycle had kicked in. However, Jon was not ready to give up the breast. I nursed him for three more months into my sixth pregnancy. The doctors were sternly telling me to stop breastfeeding. La Leche was encouraging me to nurse right up to my delivery day! The doctors were getting angry, and not being nice about it, "Stop nursing, you're 37 years old and pregnant!" I kind of knew all that. Doctor visits were getting stressful.

Then I had a dream, in it my mom was asking me if I have a girl's name picked out. Because my mom had four girls, naturally I would dream of her asking me this question. I only had boy's names chosen so far. In the dream, I tell her not yet, she tells me I need to choose one. I recall saying "If it's a girl, I will name her after Jesus Christ—Christine." I am gun shy after last time to tell anyone I have a girl's name chosen. When I awoke, I asked Al what he thought of the name Christine, he said it was fine with him. We were prepared, but I was afraid to get excited thinking this pregnancy might be a girl.

When Dr. Joseph Cudia delivered Christine, on December 28th, he said, "My wife and I should have tried one more time for a girl." He also had five sons. We were overjoyed! When Al called the house, my sister Kathy answered the phone and asked him, "Are you sure it's a girl?" Yes! And her name is Christine Lynn.

"*Find your delight in the Lord who will give you our hearts desire.*"
Ps 37:4

I don't think Christine wore anything but dresses the first five or six years of her life. When I look back on pictures, she is always all dressed up! Everyone was excited, not just me.

When Christine was two years old, the Lord blessed us again. The due date was in January 1986. I had turned forty in September, I wasn't nursing nor using birth control. I remember telling Al when we found out

I was pregnant for the seventh time, "Maybe we could call everyone from the delivery room and tell them we had a baby!"

We were happy, the hard part was telling family and friends that we were having another baby. I would think, "Please be happy for us." It was difficult telling our own children that they were going to have a new brother or sister. By this time, Tommy was in high school and Brian was graduating from eighth grade. We had just attended Brian's graduation ceremony and were on our way to Pizza Hut to celebrate. We decided to tell them in the car on the way; they were not happy campers. The older ones were angry at us and had me crying. "Not another baby!" they screamed at us. The younger ones were excited and happy, jumping with joy. What a ride in the car, actually it was a van. We had outgrown a car. To this day, Tom & Brian bring up that eventful ride to Pizza Hut, and we all get a big laugh. Not so then, not so.

It takes nine months to have a baby, I know the reason. It takes us that long to get comfortable with the idea, we needed to prepare everyone for a new addition to the family. And for us to 'prepare' the house also. We added on a second bathroom, that's right, we had only one bathroom with six children. We had four bedrooms, so it was just a matter of shifting who slept where.

I knew that once again I would be bombarded with all the negative comments and disdainful looks. I wanted to have a response ready that would nicely shut them up. One morning while I was reading my Bible, I asked the Lord to give me a word, "How can I respond to those who verbally attack me?" I opened the bible and read ***"But Jesus remained silent; he made no reply."*** **Mk 14:61**

This scripture referenced when Jesus was brought before the Sanhedrin, questioned as to the false accusations against him. I looked up all four of the gospels, Jesus was silent. Period. Even when the soldiers spit on Him and cursed Him. Silence. That was God's answer. And it was so freeing. Say nothing, I do not have to defend myself to anyone. Al and I were happy, we were providing for our children, we had a good family life, and more importantly, we were in God's will.

It wasn't long before I needed to put this into practice. A friend from church came over and when I answered the door, she noticed I was pregnant, commenting, "Don't you have television?" I just smiled and didn't say a word. You know what happened? She backed right down, telling me what a good mother I was. How happy she was for me. It was a good lesson I learned that day. I did not have to defend myself for being blessed. This is how God was blessing me and my husband. Not everyone is meant to have seven children and I will never judge someone on their family size.

Due to my high risk pregnancy with Christine, I was not looking forward to the speech from the doctors. The speeches turned into threats and one doctor in the practice even said, "Your baby could be born dead," and that I should be prepared for it. He was trying to force me into having an amniocentesis, which can be harmful to the baby. I told him no matter what happens, I was trusting in God and I was not going to put my baby at risk. This test could cause a miscarriage. He said my attitude was refreshing to hear, however in his 'personal opinion', I should take the test. The other doctors in the practice told me not to listen to him. I didn't intend to listen.

On February 9th, 1986, Melissa Renee was born through an emergency C-section. Her heartbeat would fade during a contraction and we discovered the umbilical cord was around her neck. The C-section saved her life. We were so happy that Melissa was healthy and now Christine would have a sister.

There were four doctors in the OBGYN practice. The one who was on call that day was the doctor who had scared me about my age and argued with me on every visit. After she was born, he came into the hospital room and apologized for coming down so hard on me. Years later, I came to work at the same OBGYN office where the four doctors were still practicing. My girlfriend Dianne asked me, "How can you work for him after all he put you through?" Forgiveness, that's how. I had forgiven him a long time ago.

From the day, I heard the Lord's voice in my spirit, telling me He wanted to bless us with more children, to the day I delivered our seventh and last child, we trusted in the Lord and His Divine Plan. And those were some of the best years of our lives.

"Trust in the Lord with all your heart, on your own intelligence rely not; in all your ways be mindful of him, and he will make straight your paths."
Prv 3:5-6

Chapter 7

Lost and Found

Myself and Brian kissing on beach

I can remember my dad going food shopping with Kathy and Gerry, my twin sisters, they were eight years old when he left them at the Acme Market. While he shopped, they ran amuck like kids love to do. Most moms would never allow it, but dads, well that's a different story. I think most women are happy when their husbands like to shop, and my dad was one of those men. My father focused on the deed, not the kids playing tag in the aisles. He loaded up the car with the groceries and headed for home, arriving childless. When he walked in the door with groceries and no children, my mom screeched at him in panic, "Where are the twins?" I thought he had really lost his mind, not just them! Low and behold, he passed the same genetic gene down to me. Not sure what exact gene that is, but I definitely inherited it. When he returned to the Acme Market.

Kathy and Gerry were outside waiting for him to come back for them. At least they were together, maybe not as scary for them, had they been alone. I am sure my dad was relieved to see the twins, as all kinds of awful thoughts race through your head when you lose a child.

This I know from experience. I can laugh now about the stories of losing my children, but when it actually happened, it was the most dreadful feeling I had ever experienced. When you realize, a child is gone, the fear is not just mental, but physical one as well. I could feel the blood running out of my head, becoming pale whiter than white; dizzy, scared and the feeling of helplessness comes over you. Then you become hysterical, yelling their name, searching the area, it's like having an out-of-body experience. Yes, every time it was the same, it never became less frightening.

In most cases, my children wandered off on their own, but more than a few times, I was the one who wandered away from them. Brian, however, always took off on his own, and was the biggest offender. I will only share that one time Brian got lost, but it was the one that really scared us. It was the summer of 1974, and at that time we only had Tommy and Brian. It was a hot summer day at the shore, so I decided to take them to the beach in Seaside Park by myself. Tommy was playing by the perimeter of the ocean while Brian played in the sand at the edge the blanket. I kept my eyes on Tommy as he was so close to the waves and further away from me. After some time passed, Tommy came back up to the blanket and asked, "Where is Brian?" As I turned to show him where his brother was playing—no Brian! Not anywhere in sight. I knew he did not go down to the water; I would have seen him. I started calling for him, searching the beach behind our blanket, looking to see if he had wandered off to play in the sand further away. I then quickly ran to the lifeguards, describing a three-year-old in a red bathing suit, no shoes, no shirt. The said for me sitting on the beach, while they notified the other lifeguards to look for him. They assured me that they would find him easily, as he would be crying. I knew better, though. Brian, wherever he was, would not be crying. Brian would be on an adventure; a mom knows her child.

I asked another mother I had just met in my hysteria to please help me by keeping Tommy near her so I could go looking for Brian. We were at Seaside Park Beach which has a boardwalk that extends into the next town of Seaside Heights. I took off down the boardwalk, crying, calling his name and asking everyone, "Did you see a little boy in a red bathing suit, no shoes no top, no hat?" The distance from the Park to the Heights is about a mile, or ten city blocks. In the summer, the boardwalk is always busy with summer tourists, bikers and beachgoers. On the Park side, there are usually joggers and families strolling along on an old splintered boardwalk. My search headed towards Seaside Heights where the amusement rides and concession stands are located. From our blanket on the beach you can see the rides all the way down the other end of the boardwalk Knowing Brian, he had to be heading that way, he would not even look lost.

When I got to Seaside Heights, the crowds were intense, but I found him at the kiddie rides, peering through a fence surrounding the choo-choo trains, just watching all the activity. I asked him if he knew he was lost, and he said, "Yes, I heard the loud speaker man say I was lost." Oh, and by the way, he wasn't crying, only me.

Four years later, I now have three boys, AJ is two years old, Brian is seven and Tommy is nine. I was watching my sister Patty's three children, ranging in ages from five to eight years old and we were all going to the beach. This time I brought my sister Kathy with me to help me take care of the children for the day. It was a beautiful beach day, hot and muggy, not a breeze in the air. Everyone was excited! We all piled into our station wagon, with towels and toys. Back then we didn't have car seats, booster seats or seatbelts; just cram everyone into the car. To get to Seaside Beach, you have to go over the Tom Mathis Bridge; one lane in and one lane out. Normally it's a ten-minute ride, but on this very warm summer afternoon, we hit bumper-to-bumper traffic. This was going to be close to an hour ride. When we were midway across the bridge, after about a half hour into the ride; I turned around to praise AJ for being such a good boy, as he wasn't climbing back and forth over all the seats as he usually did. No AJ!

He was not even in the car! All I could remember was opening the highchair for him to jump down, as we were loading up the car. Now I was imaging him standing at the curb as we pulled away! Oh, my God, where is he? I couldn't Pull over or turn the car around on this single lane bridge going into Seaside. That awful sick feeling came over me as I realized that we left without him, and there was nothing I could do about it, helpless. No cell phones either, all I could do was pray he was all right and get over this bridge to a pay phone. I would call Al who was working across the street at the Driftwood Deli for the summer, so he could go the house and get AJ. As I looked over at my sister Kathy in disbelief, we both started laughing! Sometimes laughter is an expression of hysteria, I found out that summer afternoon.

We finally crossed the bridge, found a phone booth, and I called Al at the Deli, he had AJ with him! Thankfully, before Al would leave the house, he always checked everything, each room, lights, stove, and so on. Usually when his OCD kicked in, it would drive me crazy. That day, I was never happier for it. In checking the bedrooms, he found AJ playing on the floor by his toy box and we were long gone. Praise the Lord! Al said, "Just go to the beach, have fun, he will be fine with me." What a relief! Another lesson learned; we really need to count noses!

It seems that 'lost gene' kicks in when the kids are about three years old. When Matthew was that magical age of three, both Al and I left him in the butcher shop. The worst part is we didn't even know we left him there but we did remember we forgot to buy soda.

Here is how it all played out. Al went into the store with instructions that the children were to wait in the car with me, I was holding Jonathan on my lap in the front passenger seat. Al was just running in for a few items we didn't buy at the grocery store earlier. But Al, being a social person that he was, chatted away with everyone and the kids got impatient. One by one the children followed him into the store; first Tommy, then Brian and AJ, and of course Matthew as well. When Al came out of the butcher shop all the boys filed out after him and piled into the car. Or so we thought. After the two-minute ride home, we started unpacking the groceries. It was then we realized we forgot the soda! Al and I drove back to get the soda from the butcher shop. Al went into the store to get the soda and to his surprise they had Matthew sitting on the counter, waiting for us to come back for him! Al told me later that when he saw Matthew, he almost said, "I told you to wait in the car," when he remembered we came by ourselves this trip. When Al came out of the store carrying Matthew, I was speechless! NO way, we had left him there! Whenever we retell this story, we always say that we would have missed him at the dinner table, if we didn't forget the soda! Guilty as charged. At least this time I was not the only adult losing a child. I did thank God that night for keeping Matthew safe. Normally if we forget something at the store, we go without it; there are times like this when our actions are inspired by the Holy Spirit.

I did count noses after that. Jon did not get lost till he was ten years old. This was the scariest for me because I lost him at the top of the World Trade Center in New York City. At the time, I was coordinator for a foreign exchange student program. We were taking French students and their host families on a bus trip to the city for a tour and to take in the sites, which included the World Trade Center. We all went up to the top of the Twin Towers, where you could walk around on the outside deck to view all of New York City. The view was breath-taking.

When making arrangements for a large group, I would keep a count of each student and their host family with a checklist and set a time limit for each tour. This allowed time to gather everyone, meet the bus and move on to the next sightseeing activity. When it was time to leave the observation area, I told Jon we were leaving and I assumed he followed us, but he stayed doing his own thing. The group of about thirty people, adults and children, entered the express elevator that zooms down, nonstop to the lobby. Directly outside the World Trade Center, our bus was waiting. While I was standing in the middle of the bus taking attendance, Jonathan runs up the steps of the bus, scared, hysterical and very upset, crying out, "Mom! You left me at the top of the towers!" Well, I am sure when I completed the checklist, I would have realized he was

51

missing. Nonetheless, I felt that sickening feeling when you think of what *could* have happened. What if the bus was around the corner of the World Trade Center and not in front of the building or if we had pulled out into traffic before Jon got on the bus? It's not the same feeling you experience when you are actually searching for your child, but it is still a heart wrenching feeling. I felt so bad. Jonathan to this day, tells everyone I bought him a Yankee hat that day because I left him on the 100th floor of the World Trade Center. Guilty as charged!

Tommy, my oldest son, never got lost. He was always more fearful of being out of my sight, so he stayed close. In fact, he lives on the same street as me today, only ten houses away. I love it because I get to see my grandsons almost daily, and I have never lost one of them! Perhaps I learnt to count noses.

My youngest two, the girls; you are thinking, she would never lose them. Wrong! Christine was about eight or nine years old when I lost her in New York City at FAO Swartz, the biggest department toy store in the city. FAO Swartz is huge two-story toy store with demonstrations going on in the isles, flying airplanes, musical dolls and automated cars, trucks and trains. They even have the life-size Toy Soldiers from Babes in Toyland! With all the crowds, there is only a narrow path through the displays for customers to maneuver, this is especially true during the Christmas holidays. Our whole family was slowly weaving its way through the crowds, going from one awesome spectacular showcase to another.

Christine was fascinated with the dollhouses. Each room was exquisitely and beautifully decorated with miniature furniture and dolls. Every room told a fantasy story that every little girl could imagine, and we spent a significant amount of time there poring over each tiny room décor. As the crowd began to move on, inches at a time, so did our family. As we started to turn a corner after passing a few more displays I realised that Christine was no longer with us. Between the mob of people behind us, and the doll houses, I could not see her. I alerted the family and I was frantically looking for her between people, calling her name, trying not to step on any small children as I weaved in and out of the crowd back towards the dollhouses. I finally got there, no Christine! Then I spotted her on the lower level, she had taken the escalator down to the main entrance and was heading towards the exit doors! I started screaming at the top of my lungs, "Christine! Look up here, we're upstairs!" She heard me and stopped in her tracks. I raced down the escalator and was greeted by an angry nine-year-old, like we left her on purpose! Take a deep breath, this could have gone really bad. What if she had made it to the exit door leading outside to the street before I spotted her? I couldn't even bring myself to think about it.

The only similarity between losing Christine and losing Melissa is that they both got lost in toy stores. It was right before Halloween and I took AJ, Matt, Jon, Christine and Melissa to look for costumes at Kiddie City in Toms River. We all pretty much stayed together looking at the masks, costumes and accessories; deciding on who would be what for Halloween.

By the exit doors they have a few Playschool Houses, the kind you can set up in your backyard. They were large enough for a child to fit inside and sit at the table and pretend they are having a tea party. They can also look out the windows, answer a play telephone on the wall in the kitchen, etc. Unknown to us, my four-year-old Melissa had gone inside one of the Playhouses while we were leaving the store. At the time, I was driving our custom-made van which had long seats in the back against the van walls on each side. There were no seatbelts, or car seats, it wasn't the safest, but the set-up was perfect for seven kids.

As I pulled out of the parking lot onto the main road, AJ started yelling at me, "Mom, Melissa is not in the car!" I continued to drive, because AJ was known for playing tricks on everyone, I thought he was up to it again. But he got hysterical, screaming at me, "MELISSA IS REALLY NOT HERE!" I realized he was serious. I did a K-turn in the middle of the road, heading back as fast as this van would take me. In order to get back to Kiddie City, you have to do a U-turn at the traffic light and cross back over another major road to get to the entrance of Kiddie City. This takes a lot of added time. So, I decided to pull over and let AJ out of the car to run across the grassy meadow, in order to get to the store faster and find Melissa. I was doing this crazy insane 'road-trip' to the entrance. AJ was about fourteen years old at the time, he ran like a deer across that field.

As I came up to the entrance, AJ was walking out of the store holding Melissa's hand. He told me that when he entered the store, they were announcing my name on the loudspeaker; assuming I was still in the store! Why don't I count noses all the time? I'm blaming the 'lost gene'.

We can read about when Mary and Joseph lost Jesus,

"Not finding him, they returned to Jerusalem in search of him. On the third day, they came upon him in the temple sitting in the midst of the teachers, listening to them and asking them questions."
Lk 2:45-46

Mary and Joseph must have been panicked and frightened. Luke clearly describes them as looking for Jesus, '*With great anxiety*' vs 48. As Mitch Finley wrote in the devotional *Living Faith,* "They were probably freaking out!"

I can forgive myself for losing my children as Mary and Joseph had one child and they lost him. I am in good company.

Chapter 8

Unlimited Forgiveness

'Forgiveness is freedom'. When I first read that statement in my Living Faith devotional booklet, it was puzzling. I continued reading and Kristen Armstrong, a writer for the publication, explains forgiveness is not about the other person, it's about you. It's a gift of grace you give yourself, it is not about letting someone off the hook, but rather un-hooking yourself from past pain. Wow. I get it now.

"Peter came up and asked Jesus, 'Lord when my brother wrongs me, how often must I forgive him? Seven times?' 'No,' Jesus replied, 'Not seven times; I say seventy times seven times. My heavenly Father will treat you in exactly the same way unless each of you forgives his brother from his heart."
Mt 18:21-22, 35

As a new Christian and mom, I always tried to teach my children the same lessons I was learning. One lesson in particular that comes to mind was one morning when I had been making pancakes for Tommy, Brian and AJ. My thoughts wandered back to the night before when I stopped to get gas on my way to work. The young attendant had smart-mouthed me when I pulled up to the pump. When I asked him his name, he gave me the name of his co-worker. They both laughed hysterically, they thought it was a big joke. I was fuming! I had to get going and be in a pleasant mood when I arrived at my client's home. I put the whole thing out of my mind. Or so I thought.

The following morning while I was making breakfast, I started thinking about how rude and fresh that gas station attendant was to me the night before. Now, as I am recalling this confrontation in my mind, Brian said to me, "Mom, what does it mean in the Lord's prayer to forgive others who trespass against you?"

I looked at him and then I looked up to heaven, and said, "OK, Lord, I forgive him."

The boys were looking at me like I have just gone crazy, so I told them the story about what happened to me the night before. I explained how angry the gas station attendants had made me and how God knows all our thoughts! I always laugh when the Lord speaks through the kids, and I love that we all learn together. Forgiveness is a lesson I learn every day. We all want our children to live and learn the lesson as well.

Here is what I learned; forgiveness is not who is right and who is wrong, it is about letting go, giving it to the Lord, and asking him to help you to forgive and forget. It is not approving someone's bad behavior, allowing them to hurt you, or to stay in a close relationship with you.

Forgiving is very freeing. It can take a lot of giving the situation over to the Lord, and then realizing you have taken it back again. Finally, leaving it with the Lord and being able to forgive. When we don't forgive for whatever reason, it becomes like a cancer, it goes underground and becomes bitterness, anger or resentment. This will hurt you physically, mentally, emotionally and spiritually. Unforgiveness can block healing as well as answers to prayer; it is for our own good that God calls us to forgive one another.

During those early years, I was reading everything I could get my hands on to help me grow in faith. One day, I came across a book on forgiveness. One chapter gave the reader an exercise to do to help with the act of forgiving. For example, you are instructed to close your eyes and think of a person whom you need to forgive, even if you cannot recall the incident. You let their name come to mind, asking God to help you forgive them. I practiced this exercise and did think of different people who had hurt me. For some I remembered exactly what it was and for others, I just knew there was something between us. Suddenly, my heart started racing and I became very anxious. I had no idea what was happening to me, but the best way I can explain it, was like my mind and my heart were at odds. The struggle was that part of me did not want to hear who I needed to forgive. I quietly prayed in the spirit until I became calm. I then asked God, who do I need to forgive? Have I forgotten someone? I heard God say in my heart, I needed to forgive Him. In that instant, I knew why.

Years ago, when I was in high school, I fell in love with Don and we dated all through school. When we graduated, he asked me to marry him, and we were engaged on August 6th 1963. Three weeks later Don, his brother, Bobby, and his best friend, Joe, were killed when a train hit their pickup truck. They died instantly. Don was driving to a junk yard for car parts, the only way to reach it was through this dirt road. They had to pass over a railroad crossing that was overgrown with vegetation; there were no flashing signals, warning bells, or crossing gates that come down. They never knew what hit them.

His parents and I were devastated; their only children were dead, my future with Don was gone. His dad gave up his milk delivery business. I think he had a breakdown after their deaths. I can still hear his mom on the phone when she called my house that afternoon, "Both my boys are dead!" she cried to my mom as I was listening on the extension phone.

I don't know how I got through the viewing, grave side service and burials. Don, Bobby and Joe all had open caskets and they were waked at the same funeral parlor. The first few months after their deaths was a blur, I just remember wanting to be near his mom and dad as we grieved. I don't think my parents understood that part of my grieving. There was no therapy offered then or bereavement groups so, you just went from one day to the next. I did call my church and spoke to a priest, I had so many questions about heaven and dying. Looking back, I know now that I got through those first months with God's grace. We all know bad things do happen to good people.

His parents and I remained very close through the years. They even came to Al and my wedding, and years later my children called them Aunt Dot and Uncle Ed. Our children all knew my story, and we would visit Dot and Ed regularly. We would take the kids to the cemetery to visit Don's grave. Today, they are all together in heaven.

I thought I had forgiven God for Don's death. I met Al, fell in love, got married and together we had a wonderful family. Not realizing that deep down, a part of my heart was hardened towards God. We cannot hide anything from Him, He knows our innermost thoughts, our pain and our joys. He loves us, and wants us to be free, healed and restored so we can love one another. In order to be able to love fully, we need to forgive. Sometimes the person we need to forgive is God. Sometimes it is others or ourselves.

Remember the doctor from Melissa's delivery who apologized to me for coming down so hard on me about being pregnant at 40? (Ch. 6). Eventually, I was able to forgive him. Forgiveness didn't happen immediately, or easily, it took a lot of time and prayer. But the forgiveness was so total that I was able to work for him years later.

At one retreat that I attended a few years ago, the presenters gave us an exercise to do when someone hurts you or someone close to you, and you're having a very difficult time forgiving them. They said to bring that person to Jesus. Visualize taking them to Him and tell Jesus how you feel about what happened; the disappointment, the pain, anger, etc. Leave the person and the situation with Jesus to take care of, and ***back*** away from them. I found that when I backed away, leaving them with Jesus it really helped me. Later, when the hurt would creep back into my thoughts, I would think, *This is no longer my problem, its's in Jesus' hands and He is taking care of it.* Freedom!

> ***Never forget the three powerful***
> ***resources you always have available***
> ***to you: love, prayer, and forgiveness.***
> **H. Jackson Brown, Jr.**

Chapter 9
Tithing

I attended many Catholic Charismatic Prayer Meetings over the years, I always came away so filled with joy and knowledge of the working of the Holy Spirit. The uplifting music, fellowship and the people's sharing always had Al and I coming back each week wanting more.

One of my favorite parts of prayer meeting was when people shared their personal stories about how God was working in their lives. This one evening, we had two guest speakers, Sal and Dee Grasso, to share their personal testimony and speak on the scriptural principle of tithing. Sal played a guitar and Dee did most of the sharing about their life in Christ. You could see and hear how much in love they were with each other, as well as their passionate love for Jesus. It just shone through them as they spoke. It was truly delightful to see. Their sharing on tithing was, for many, a tough pill to swallow.

Tithing; a new word for me. This was the first time I heard a teaching on it. The teaching was different then when a priest or minister stand up in church asking for donations or requesting more money in the collections each week.

Sal and Dee spoke of the Scriptures, where there are written promises and consequences for not taking care of the poor and needy.

"He who shuts his ear to the cry of the poor will himself also call and not be heard."
Prv 21:13

"Refuse no one the good on which he has a claim when it is in your power to do it for him. Say not to your neighbor go and come again tomorrow when you can do it at once."
Prv 3:27-28

From that evening, many who attended began to tithe. Tithing was a scriptural charge, that as Catholics we were not familiar. Sal and Dee's teachings were a blessing for all who wanted to be obedient to God's word. Tithing has been called 'The Law of Reciprocity' the principle of sowing and reaping, what you sow, you also reap.

One Friday evening before prayer meeting, a few weeks after this teaching, Al and I were going over our bills. We were short $50.00 to pay our utility bill. It was fresh in our minds, and not something we wanted to be stressing about at the meeting. We decided to put it out of our minds and enjoy the prayer time we always enjoyed.

We began as usual, singing a few uplifting songs, listening to scripture readings, and praising the Lord. That was another one of my favorite things about prayer groups meeting; the praise and worship. You receive such a calmness and inner peace when you worship and focus on Jesus, it was easy to forget about our money problem.

After prayer meeting, we stayed to have coffee, cake and fellowship. That was when our friend Bob Fuggi approached Al and said quietly to him, "The Lord told me before I came here tonight to give you this." He handed Al money, and without looking at how much it was, Al put it in his pocket. He gave Bob a hug and whispered in his ear, "Thank you brother." I am sure Al felt uncomfortable. Sometimes it's easier to give than to receive. When we got home, Al took the money out of his pocket and there was a fifty dollar bill! Bob's tithing money. I don't believe in coincidences; I believe in God 'incidences'.

Bob was a strong Christian and a very successful businessman. He had been a born-again Christian for many years, and tithing was a natural part of his life. As one of the long-established leaders, he had always sought the direction of the Holy Spirit beforehand, to guide and bless the meeting.

It was during that prayer time God gave him the word to give Al the fifty dollars. This night God used his tithing to meet our need. As Bob was a very successful businessman, his giving to others was measured back to him one-hundredfold.

"Give and gifts will be given to you; a good measure packed together, shaken down, and over-flowing, will be poured into your lap. For the measure with which you measure will in return be measured out to you."
Lk 6:38

Mary Crowley, the founder of Home Interiors, was a born-again Christian and a generous woman. Mary would always say, "You can't out give God, for he has a bigger shovel." Around her neck, she wore a tiny gold shovel and if anyone would ask her about its significance, she would tell them about tithing.

I think it's important to be open to the promptings of God's Spirit, when it comes to giving, because we cannot give to every cause. When I feel a stirring within me to give, I know I need to pay attention to it. When I donate, I keep these principles in mind:

"The willingness to give should accord with one's means, not go beyond them." **2 Cor 8:12** *"Everyone must give according to what he has inwardly decided; not sadly, not grudgingly, for God loves a cheerful giver."*
2 Cor 9:7

Tithing is more than about giving money. Tithing is also giving your time and using your gifts to help others. One lesson I was able to teach the children when they were young, was about giving food not only when there is a food drive, or to soup kitchens; in other words, not just to the needy but as a kindness as well. Our neighbor at the time was Mr. Cristofoli, an elderly gentleman who had recently lost his wife, there was no other family and he was lonely. One day I baked a zucchini bread for him and Tom and Brian came with me to pay him a visit. He was very touched by our visit and he loved the bread!

Later that evening, there was a knock on our door and Joanne Marino, a friend of mine, had come to give us a large tray of cookies! Her family had been at a celebration and this delicious looking tray of cookies was left over! Joanne knowing how our boys would love the cookies and brought the tray to our house. The very same night that we gave a loaf of bread to a neighbor, God provided through Joanne, even a bigger gift to my children! Cookies! His shovel is bigger and so is His heart!

There are times like this when God allows us to see immediately the benefit of His promises. There are times when you give; you will not see the results right away or at all. Giving is also about treating others how you would want to be treated and doing the right thing when the opportunity arises. And it goes both ways; not to be too proud to ask for help when we are in need too. I learned a lot of valuable life-long lessons on tithing, about giving and receiving. I learned about God's promises and His love for us and for sure I learned life-long lesson on tithing.

My prayer at that time, when they were young children, was that they would take it to heart about sharing and treating others with compassion and respect. Not only learning those lessons but living them as well. Today, as young adults, I see that their lives have reflected those qualities. My prayers were answered. I feel very blessed to have all my children living those lessons very well. I thank God for the choices they have made in life.

Chapter 10

Where Are They Now?

From wedding, just my children

Whenever I see on Facebook, a stairway to heaven and the caption 'If only Heaven had visiting hours', I think of Al. This is how I would imagine my visit with Al would take place if heaven really had visiting hours.

Just beyond the stairway, I see him. Such a rush comes over me. It's been so long, but I know it's just a visit. I see the excitement in Al's expression! As he comes towards me, I notice his walk is the same as I remember; throwing his feet out to the side. A feeling of comfort comes over me, I can do this, without crying or fainting.

AL: "Lynn, let's sit down and talk."

Me: "How long do we have?"

AL: "Lynn, as long as you need."

Me: "Great! I told the children I was getting a heavenly visit. I asked each of them what they wanted me to share.

"Since Tommy is our oldest, I will start with him. Before I begin, Al, I just want you to know how Tom visits the cemetery often. They all miss you a lot. Tommy is still working for Mutual of Omaha. Can you believe he now has over 700 clients? The most rewarding part for him is building relationships with the customers and their families. He really cares about his clients, much like you cared about your students every year.

"Our grandsons, Andrew, Blake and Antonio are growing up to be fine young men.

"Brian is doing what he loves! Being creative every day; doing marketing for BMW group and MINI. He and Nina and our granddaughter Sophie visit me often. Our house remains their getaway in the summer, a reprieve from the hot humid days in Teaneck. Brian is a good provider and a great dad just like you were. Together we raised some pretty awesome children, and they are doing the same!

"Al, guess where AJ is? He is on a 'mission' he calls it *The Endless Summer*. He is filming on all the islands in Hawaii for a real estate show on HGTV. God has blessed AJ with the gift of photography. He has such a unique talent for taking pictures that just draw you right into the scene. I am so grateful I can share with you these events, even if it's just for these moments together. I miss this the most, sharing our thoughts and prayers for our children. There are times when I think, *I can't wait to get home and tell Al*. And then I remember.

"Matthew is still living in California, eighteen years now! He is working for Fuse Design Agency in Laguna Beach. He was promoted to Creative Design Director, responsible for creating websites and advertisements for corporate companies.

"Matt takes after you Al; with his love for fishing and hunting, he has traveled to Utah and Montana, pursuing both loves. He is definitely living your dream. Matt and AJ are still single and Jonathan too, but you know me, I am still praying they meet that special someone. The boys all seem to be enjoying being single. I just know my life would never have been as fulfilled and happy had I not met you. They know we just want happiness for them too.

"All the boys are great cooks, just like you were. And, just as you were a great family man, I know they will be too. You were a wonderful role model for our sons. Remember the smell of those Good Friday meals you always cooked for us, the aroma of seafood wafting through the kitchen? The mussels, octopus and the hot garlic bread in the oven! Now, AJ has been our dedicated chef and he learned all from you, perfectly!

"Jonathan is living the dangerous life as a police officer in Dunellen. I just found out recently they call Dunellen the 'miracle mile' because there is so much in that mile! Movie theater, ice rink, train station and several bars. Although Dunellen is a relatively safe town, some of the surrounding areas are gang affiliated causing his job to be more dangerous.

"Jon is a caring and devoted police officer. I am sure you are very proud of him too. You always had a respect for law enforcement and I really believe, looking back, you were one of the motivating factors for his career choice.

"Jon owns a home in Beachwood and his dog Boomer is the sweetest Pit/Boxer anyone could find. And to think he was a rescue dog! I guess in a lot of ways Jon is in the 'Rescue Business'.

"Christine is the only one to follow in your career footsteps. She is still teaching at Morgan Elementary School in Hamilton, NJ and tutoring on the side. She is also a new homeowner, living in Hamilton. Chris loves teaching, just as you did Al! She is enjoying those times when students have those *'Ah-ah Moments'* when the lesson finally clicks! Her days are filled with laughter, humor, exhaustion, and every so often, tears! Sometimes it is Christine and sometimes it is one of her students. I am so proud to see how hard she works and how motivated she has become. Still single. I guess she is following in her big brother's footsteps.

"Al, I often wonder if we set the bar too high. We loved each other till the end and had a happy and fulfilling life together with our children. I want them to know our relationship was also a work in progress. Together we tried to be sensitive to each other's needs. You were always the best at that Al.

"Melissa, our 'baby', shortly after finishing college, moved out to Southern California to find her career. Well it worked! Melissa has been the Director of Sales and Corporate Events, at the Hotel La Casa del Camino, in Laguna Beach.

"I love seeing how Melissa and Matthew spend their weekends together since they live so close. After Mass, they sometimes brunch with mutual friends, spend an afternoon at the beach or some other fun activity. They call it '*Fun Day Sunday*!'

Full wedding photo of entire family

"Melissa has met a great guy; Dave Anderson, you would really like Dave, he fits right into our family. He also has a close-knit family and is the oldest of four. The Andersons are personable and friendly, just like us! Dave is a hard worker and will be a good provider, and guess what else? Dave wants at least four children! Melissa is blessed to have him. And he, her. The wedding date is set for October 2017 in California. All of our sons will dance with her for you, and I am walking her down the aisle for us. But still we all selfishly wish you could be the one giving Melissa away and the one who dances with her."

I just don't want this visit to end…somehow, I am back here…sitting at my kitchen table. There was so much more I wanted to tell Al; like how Jon has vivid dreams of him, the comfort we get from the 'signs', the hummingbirds, the rainbows, the songs. I recall the scripture, ***"In the time of their visitation they shall shine, and shall dart about as sparks through stubble."*** **Wis 3:7**

I was led to write this for our children so they would have the story of how our family became and grew. How grateful I am to God, our Savior, for the many blessings He bestowed on our family. It is also written in memory of Albert, who was a strong Christian man, a loving husband, father, son, uncle and friend. To pen our story of the joy we received in having a heart for seven children, raising them on a modest income, in a home filled with laughter, faith and seasoned with lots and lots of love.

What am I doing now? Taking one day at a time, trusting in the Lord with this new chapter in my life.

"Attend my people, to my teaching: listen to the words of my mouth. I will open my mouth in story. Drawing lessons from of old. We have heard them, we know them: our ancestors have recited them to us. We do not keep them from our children; we recite them to the next generation, the praiseworthy and mighty deeds of the Lord, the wonders that he performed."
Ps 7